Ayudantes de la comunidad / Helping the Community

¿Qué hacen LOS BOMBEROS?
What Do FIREFIGHTERS Do?

Amy B. Rogers

Traducido por Eida de la Vega

PowerKiDS press.

New York

Published in 2016 by The Rosen Publishing Group, Inc.
29 East 21st Street, New York, NY 10010

First Edition

Editor: Katie Kawa
Book Design: Katelyn Heinle
Spanish Translator: Eida de la Vega

Photo Credits: Cover (firefighter), pp. 1, 21, 24 (helmet) Kris Timken/Blend Images/Getty Images; cover (hands) bymandesigns/Shutterstock.com; back cover Zffoto/Shutterstock.com; p. 5 Bob Peterson/UpperCut Images/Getty Images; p. 6 Johnny Habell/Shutterstock.com; p. 9 © iStockphoto.com/AlexSava; pp. 10, 24 (hose) Klesz/Shutterstock.com; pp. 13, 24 (ladder) © iStockphoto.com/christopherarndt; p. 14 potowizard/Shutterstock.com; p. 17 karelnoppe/Shutterstock.com; p. 18 Bplanet/Shutterstock.com; p. 22 bikeriderlondon/Shutterstock.com.

Library of Congress Cataloging-in-Publication Data

Rogers, Amy B.
What do firefighters do? = ¿Qué hacen los bomberos? / by Amy B. Rogers.
p. cm. — (Helping the community = Ayudantes de la comunidad)
Parallel title: Ayudantes de la comunidad.
In English and Spanish.
Includes index.
ISBN 978-1-4994-0639-9 (library binding)
1. Fire fighters — Juvenile literature. 2. Fire extinction — Juvenile literature. I. Rogers, Amy B. II. Title.
TH9148.R589 2016
628.9'25'092 —d23

Manufactured in the United States of America

CPSIA Compliance Information: Batch #WS15PK: For Further Information contact Rosen Publishing, New York, New York at 1-800-237-9932

CONTENIDO

CONTENTS

Los bomberos apagan fuegos.

Firefighters put out fires.

Cuando hay un fuego,
los bomberos tienen que
moverse con rapidez.

Firefighters have to move quickly
when there is a fire.

Llegan al lugar del fuego
en un camión de bomberos.

They go to fires in a fire truck.

Los bomberos usan **mangueras** para apagar los fuegos.

- -

Firefighters use **hoses** to put water on fires.

Los bomberos también usan **escaleras**. Las escaleras los ayudan a alcanzar lugares altos.

Firefighters use **ladders**, too. Ladders help them get to high places.

Los bomberos ayudan a sacar a la gente de edificios en llamas.

Firefighters help people get out of burning buildings.

Los bomberos usan trajes
especiales. Estos trajes
los protegen.

Firefighters wear special clothes.
The clothes keep them safe.

También usan botas.

They also wear boots.

Los bomberos usan **cascos** para protegerse la cabeza.

Firefighters wear **helmets** to keep their head safe.

¡Los bomberos son valientes!

Firefighters are brave!

PALABRAS QUE DEBES APRENDER
WORDS TO KNOW

(los) cascos
helmets

(la) manguera
hose

(la) escalera
ladder

ÍNDICE / INDEX

SITIOS DE INTERNET / WEBSITES

Due to the changing nature of Internet links, PowerKids Press has developed an online list of websites related to the subject of this book. This site is updated regularly. Please use this link to access the list: www.powerkidslinks.com/htc/fire